MILITARY ★★★
★★★ ANIMALS

BY: LAURIE CALKHOVEN

Scholastic Inc.

CONTENTS ★★★

INTRODUCTION ★★★

Animals have fought side by side with soldiers since ancient times. You've probably heard about brave warhorses and heroic dogs, but some of the other animals in this book will surprise you!

From the tiny glowworm to the mighty elephant, animals have captured the enemy, kept soldiers safe, and been loyal friends in desperate, dangerous moments.

Discover dolphins who search for hidden mines under the sea, pigeons who were soldiers' only form of communication behind enemy lines, honeybees who seek out explosives with their antennae, and even monkeys who protect birds and airplanes from high in the treetops of China.

Whether by land, by air, or by sea, these incredible military animals will amaze you with their courage and their loyalty. Throughout history, they have been some of our bravest soldiers in times of war and our friends in times of peace.

MULES ★★★

Mules, the offspring of female horses and male donkeys, have some of the best qualities of both species. They are more patient and less likely to stumble on rough and rocky ground than horses. They are also smarter and faster than donkeys. It's no wonder that they've long been used by the military to carry food, weapons, and other supplies.

During the American Civil War, the Union army in the North used as many as one million mules. They hauled food, supplies, and **ammunition** into battle zones and often carried wounded soldiers back out again. In fact, mules are credited with helping the Union win an important **skirmish** during the Battle of Gettysburg—the bloodiest battle in the entire Civil War.

These brave animals were also called into duty in World War I. The United States and its allies used as many as 300,000 mules, and the animals found themselves in the middle of the action. Ships carrying mules were often the targets of attacks by German submarines because the enemy knew how valuable they were.

MULES ARE STRONG ANIMALS THAT CAN CARRY HEAVY LOADS ACROSS LONG DISTANCES.

GEORGE WASHINGTON'S MULES

George Washington was one of the first Americans to breed a herd of mules. Their father was a donkey named Royal Gift, which Washington received as a gift from the king of Spain.

WORLD WAR II MULE TRAINS FOLLOWED STEEP, ROCKY TRAILS TO DELIVER SUPPLIES TO US TROOPS ON THE FRONT LINES.

Mules were used during the war for hauling wagons loaded with as much as 3,000 pounds of cargo. Six mules pulled each wagon. In areas where wagons couldn't pass through, trains of fifty or more mules, carrying 250 pounds each, could travel sixty miles in a day.

During World War II, mules were called upon once again. They were able to travel through the steep mountainous areas of northern Italy as well as the dense jungles of Burma and the desert regions of North Africa—places trucks, jeeps, tanks, and even horses couldn't reach.

Today, marines are trained to use mules on missions in the mountains of Afghanistan. In steep, remote mountain areas, mules are even more valuable than **Humvees** and helicopters. ★★★

BEARS ★★★

In all of history, there's only one mention of a soldier bear. He was a private in the Polish army in World War II.

Voytek (also spelled Wojtek and pronounced VOY-tek) was just a baby brown bear who had lost his mother when a Polish military unit found him in Iran in 1943. The bear was so young that the soldiers had to feed him condensed milk. Soon, he was six feet tall and weighed 500 pounds!

Voytek enjoyed wrestling with his human buddies and even learned to salute. One of his favorite things to do was swim. And in the hot summer, he learned how to work the shower. After that, the soldiers had to lock the bathhouse to keep Voytek from using up all their water! Once, someone left the door ajar and Voytek quickly slipped inside, much to the surprise of an Arab spy who had come to steal weapons. Voytek became a hero and was given his favorite drink as a reward.

When the Polish unit learned that they were going to sail to Europe to fight with the British, they wanted to bring Voytek along. The only way to get him on the ship was to make him a soldier. Voytek was officially **drafted** into the Polish army with a name, rank, and serial number.

VOYTEK

VOYTEK WASN'T JUST A FRIEND TO THE SOLDIERS IN HIS UNIT. HE WAS A BIG HELP WHEN IT WAS TIME TO LOAD TRUCKS. HE EVEN CARRIED AMMO TO THE MEN ON THE FRONT LINES.

During the Battle of Monte Cassino in Italy, Voytek became used to the sounds of planes and exploding bombs. He bravely carried ammunition to soldiers under fire.

After the war, Voytek marched through the streets of Glasgow, Scotland, with his Polish unit. There he carried logs to the cookhouse, moved crates, and rolled barrels. When the unit returned to Poland, Voytek stayed in Scotland and went to live at the Edinburgh Zoo. His former soldier buddies often visited him and brought him presents.

★ ★ ★

WHAT'S IN A NAME?
The name Voytek means "he who enjoys war" or "smiling warrior."

VOYTEK AT THE EDINBURGH ZOO IN SCOTLAND.

CATS ★★★

Cats have played an important role on navy ships throughout history. They are responsible for keeping rats and mice from taking over and eating the sailors' food, chewing through ropes, and spreading disease aboard ships. Some sailors even believe that cats bring good luck—especially black cats.

During the Crimean War, in 1854, British and French troops occupied the Russian port town of Sevastopol. The troops were starving but couldn't find the food that Russian forces had hidden all along the waterfront. A cat known as Crimean Tom led the British and French troops to the hidden food and kept them alive. Tom wasn't an official soldier, but he was named a **mascot**. When the troops returned home to England, they brought Tom with them.

Another cat, Able Seacat Simon, served on the British Royal Navy's HMS *Amethyst* beginning in 1948. He started out as an ordinary rat catcher. Then Simon was injured during a battle on the Yangtze River in China. Not only did he survive his wounds, but Simon came back to save the ship, which had been overrun by rats. When he died, Simon was buried with full military honors.

ABLE SEACAT SIMON

SIMON IS THE ONLY CAT EVER TO WIN GREAT BRITAIN'S DICKIN MEDAL. THE MEDAL HONORS ANIMALS THAT SHOWED GREAT COURAGE WHILE SERVING IN MILITARY CONFLICTS.

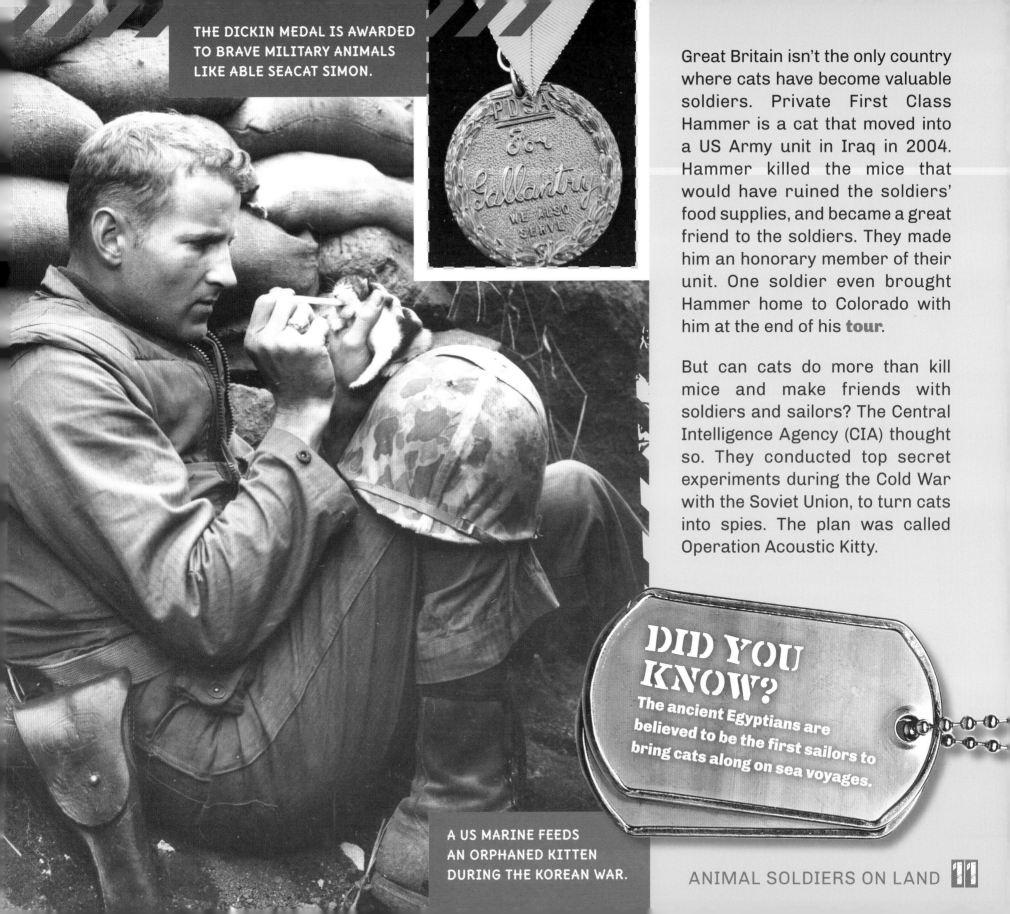

Great Britain isn't the only country where cats have become valuable soldiers. Private First Class Hammer is a cat that moved into a US Army unit in Iraq in 2004. Hammer killed the mice that would have ruined the soldiers' food supplies, and became a great friend to the soldiers. They made him an honorary member of their unit. One soldier even brought Hammer home to Colorado with him at the end of his **tour**.

But can cats do more than kill mice and make friends with soldiers and sailors? The Central Intelligence Agency (CIA) thought so. They conducted top secret experiments during the Cold War with the Soviet Union, to turn cats into spies. The plan was called Operation Acoustic Kitty.

DID YOU KNOW?

The ancient Egyptians are believed to be the first sailors to bring cats along on sea voyages.

A US MARINE FEEDS AN ORPHANED KITTEN DURING THE KOREAN WAR.

THE COLD WAR

There were not any actual battles during the Cold War, but the United States and the Soviet Union were distrustful and unfriendly (or "cold") to each other. The United States wanted to keep the Soviet Union from spreading its communist form of government around the world.

A CAT SHOWS PRIDE FOR HIS COUNTRY BY WEARING A RIBBON WITH THE NATIONAL COLORS OF UKRAINE.

In 1961, the CIA implanted a microphone in a cat's ear and a battery in its body. The cat's tail became the antenna. The plan was to have the cat eavesdrop on Soviet conversations from park benches and windowsills.

After five years of training, the cat was ready for a test. The CIA drove the spy cat to a Soviet compound in Washington, DC, and let it loose. Unfortunately, the cat was hit by a taxi. Cats may be sly and secretive like spies, but they tend to wander off. Operation Acoustic Kitty was abandoned in 1967, and not one cat had been turned into a spy. ★★★

MONKEYS ★★★

The Chinese military has a secret weapon: It's a monkey! For years, birds caused trouble at a Chinese air base. The base was right in the path of **migrating** birds. When birds fly near airplanes, they can get sucked into a plane's engines and cause a crash. Not only were birds' lives in danger, but so were those of the pilots.

The Chinese tried lots of ways to keep the birds from nesting in the trees around the base. They put up scarecrows and set off firecrackers. They sent soldiers up into the trees to knock down the nests. But the birds kept coming back—until China brought in their monkey army.

Macaque monkeys were trained to answer to whistle commands and climb into the treetops and remove the bird nests. The monkeys left behind a scent on the branches that kept the birds from coming back.

Planes, and their pilots, were once again free to fly. ★★★

MACAQUE MONKEYS, WITH TWENTY-TWO DIFFERENT SPECIES WORLDWIDE, ARE THE MOST WIDESPREAD PRIMATES ON EARTH, BESIDES HUMANS.

CAMELS ★★★

Camels have taken part in military combat in the Middle East and North Africa since ancient times. These tough animals are built to survive in the harsh desert climate, where they can carry heavy loads for long distances without food and water.

In the mid-1800s, camels were part of an experiment in the United States. The country was expanding westward and settlers needed the help of animals that could survive long journeys in the desert. On May 14, 1856, the first of what would eventually be sixty-six camels sailed across the Atlantic Ocean from North Africa all the way to Texas. For the next few years, the camels carried supplies to the army on the southwestern frontier.

Civil War broke out in the United States in 1861, and Confederate troops in the South gained control of the camels. They used them to haul food and other supplies. After the war, most of the camels were sold to zoos and carnivals.

BACTRIAN CAMELS, LIKE THE ONE PICTURED HERE, HAVE TWO HUMPS AND ARE ABLE TO SURVIVE IN BOTH HOT AND COLD CLIMATES.

CAMEL TRAINS, LIKE THIS ONE IN CHINA, HAVE CARRIED SUPPLIES AND EQUIPMENT IN WAR SINCE ANCIENT TIMES.

In World War I, a British general formed the Imperial Camel Corps to help drive the enemy out of the desert. Camels carried food, medical supplies, ammunition, and most important, water to soldiers in the field. The water they carried saved thousands of lives. ★★★

GET BACK HERE!

Camels are generally calm when under enemy fire, but they can be trouble-makers at other times. Not only do they have a habit of running away, but they often bite the kneecaps of the men riding them!

GERBILS ★★★

Can gerbils fight in the war against spies and **terrorists**? That's what Great Britain's MI5 (their version of the CIA) wanted to find out. During the 1970s, they thought that trained gerbils might be able to sniff out terrorists flying into Great Britain.

They weren't the first to get the idea. Israeli security forces tried putting cages of specially trained gerbils at airport security checks. Fans nearby blew the scent of passengers into the gerbils' cages. When humans are stressed out, they release a chemical called adrenaline. Gerbils, with their strong sense of smell, were trained to press a lever if they detected high levels of adrenaline coming from a passenger.

Unfortunately, it turns out that people who are afraid of flying are just as stressed out in airports as potential terrorists. Israel gave up on the experiment, and Great Britain never gave the terrorist-sniffing gerbils a test. ★★★

GERBILS WERE STATIONED NEAR AIRPORT SECURITY TO SNIFF OUT POSSIBLE TERRORISTS.

PIGS ★★★

PIGS, IN ADDITION TO SCARING ELEPHANTS, HAVE HELPED THE MILITARY KEEP SOLDIERS SAFE.

Pigs haven't always been treated well by soldiers. In ancient Rome, soldiers would starve pigs for days and then let them loose in enemy camps. The hungry pigs would eat everything in their path, leaving the enemy soldiers weak without food.

Pigs were also used in battle against elephants. Those great beasts were terrified by squeals from even the smallest pigs. When Romans were attacked by war elephants, they covered pigs in tar and set them on fire. The poor pigs were then driven toward the elephants, setting off a stampede. The elephants, in their terror to get away, trampled many of their own soldiers.

Things haven't gotten much better for pigs in modern times. The US military has used pigs to test how well body armor will hold up in bomb blasts, and British army doctors have used pigs for battlefield surgery training.

Pigs have helped scientists learn valuable information that keeps soldiers safe, but animal rights groups have asked the military to stop using pigs in their testing. ★★★

ELEPHANTS ★★

What would you do if an enormous beast with giant tusks was bearing down on you? You'd run, of course! That's exactly what ancient Roman soldiers did the first time they saw elephants. General Pyrrhus built up a large army of elephants and used them to invade Italy in 280 BC. Roman soldiers and horses, seeing the giant elephants charge, panicked and ran.

Sixty years later, Hannibal, one of history's great military commanders, famously marched over the Alps and Pyrenees Mountains in 218 BC to attack the Romans. With him were thousands of soldiers and thirty-seven elephants. By this point the Romans had learned a bit about dealing with elephants, and eventually Hannibal was defeated.

Before gunpowder was invented, some Asian armies built large wooden towers that could stand on top of an elephant's back. These towers held as many as thirty **archers** who let their arrows fly while riding atop the powerful animals.

IN ANCIENT ROME, ELEPHANTS WENT INTO BATTLE AND EVEN WORE THEIR OWN ARMOR!

Elephants are still useful in modern warfare, even if they no longer go directly into battle. During World War II, elephants helped the **Allies** build bridges and roads in the jungles of Burma. They were able to balance huge logs with their tusks, hoist them in the air, and carefully set them down exactly where they needed to go.

ELEPHANTS ON THE HOME FRONT

The British army used so many horses and mules in World War I that there was a serious shortage of animal workers at home. A circus elephant named Lizzie stepped in to help. She hauled as much scrap metal as three horses. Other elephants plowed fields, hauled crops, and carried heavy loads.

Elephants became so valuable during World War II that when warning came of a Japanese attack, the British moved their elephants to make sure they wouldn't fall into the hands of the enemy. Forty-seven elephants were marched over nearly impassible mountain tracks. One elephant named Bandoola was looked upon by the others as their commanding officer and led all of his followers to safety. When it was over, Bandoola broke into a pineapple grove and ate 900 pineapples!

During the Vietnam War, a Special Forces captain flew two elephants to a remote mountain village . . . by helicopter!

US Special Forces recruited and trained Vietnamese soldiers from the mountain villages and used lumber to build training camps for them. The local forests were rich in trees, so the army bought a used sawmill and trained villagers to make lumber. But getting logs from the jungle to the sawmill destroyed army vehicle after army vehicle. That's when the village elders came up with the idea of using elephants. The only problem? There were no elephants in the area. So the United States bought two elephants from a village more than 300 miles away.

HERDS OF ELEPHANTS CARRIED SOLDIERS AND SUPPLIES THROUGH THE JUNGLE TO PLACES TANKS COULDN'T REACH.

HANNIBAL AND HIS ARMY CROSSED THE RHONE RIVER TO ATTACK ROME BY WAY OF THE ALPS.

ASIAN ELEPHANT

AFRICAN ELEPHANT

ASIAN OR AFRICAN ELEPHANTS?

Asian elephants are smaller than African elephants. They are also friendlier and easier to train. Historians don't know for sure what kinds of elephants were used in ancient warfare, but it is likely they were the more bad-tempered African elephants.

The two three-ton elephants (that's 6,000 pounds each!) were given medicine to keep them calm and were loaded into an airplane for a 300-mile trip to the nearest airfield. Then they were wrapped in cargo nets and suspended from a pair of helicopters. They flew the final 65 miles over the mountains to the tiny village clearing and landed safely.

The soldiers who flew them jokingly called the mission Operation Barroom. "*Barroom*" is the sound an elephant makes when it has gas! ★★★

RATS ★★★

Dogs may be man's best friend, but when it comes to sniffing out land mines, rats might be even better to have around. The African giant pouched rat has been used to detect land mines and bombs in Africa. Since 2000, hundreds of trained rats have discovered 1,500 buried land mines in Tanzania, and nearly 7,000 land mines and 1,000 bombs across Mozambique.

It's no wonder that the US Army took notice. They're now training African rodents to find mines and other explosive devices.

Rats are much lighter than dogs, so they can step on mines without setting them off. They can also scurry into tight places that dogs could never reach.

A GIANT POUCHED RAT SEARCHES FOR UNEXPLODED LAND MINES.

RATS WORK FOR FOOD. THEIR FAVORITE IS BANANAS!

All of this might just make a rat a soldier's *new* best friend. Can you imagine if one day a pet rat is issued to every soldier, along with a uniform and boots? Just don't forget the bananas! ★★★

SEARCH AND RESCUE

Rats are being trained to do more than sniff out explosives. Like dogs, they can be taught to locate humans who may be trapped after disasters such as earthquakes and tornadoes.

DOGS ★★★

For as long as humans have been fighting wars, dogs have been fighting at their sides. The ancient Romans used guard dogs to protect their armies. So did Attila the Hun. In the United States, dogs have participated in every war from the American Revolution to the modern conflicts in Iraq and Afghanistan.

In World War I, a bull terrier mix named Sergeant Stubby became famous after he participated in seventeen battles with the 102nd Infantry 26th Yankee Division. Stubby had been adopted at a training camp in Connecticut and smuggled aboard a ship bound for Europe. He learned to warn his company when poison gas attacks were on the way, and he often searched for wounded soldiers when the noise of battle calmed down. He was wounded himself more than once, but he always returned to the trenches.

SERGEANT STUBBY

SERGEANT STUBBY, THE MOST DECORATED WAR DOG OF WORLD WAR I, WAS THE ONLY DOG TO BE PROMOTED TO SERGEANT THROUGH COMBAT.

DOGS DID MORE THAN RAISE SOLDIERS' SPIRITS; THEY HELPED IN THE FIGHT AGAINST THE ENEMY. CHIPS WAS REWARDED WITH MEDALS FOR HIS BRAVERY, BUT HE WAS PROBABLY HAPPIER TO GET ANOTHER KIND OF REWARD—DOUGHNUTS!

CHIPS

Stubby was promoted to sergeant after catching a German spy—he held on to the enemy soldier's pants with his teeth until help arrived— and came home after the war to a hero's welcome. He led parades and even met three presidents: Woodrow Wilson, Warren G. Harding, and Calvin Coolidge.

While Stubby was the star of World War I, a German shepherd mix named Chips became the most decorated dog soldier in World War II. When Italian soldiers started shooting at Chips and his human handler in Sicily, Chips launched himself on the enemy, biting and barking until they surrendered. Chips was wounded, but that didn't stop him from helping to take ten more prisoners that day. General Dwight D. Eisenhower, who later became president of the United States, personally thanked Chips for his brave service. He was awarded a Silver Star for valor and a Purple Heart for his wounds.

SEA DOGS

Dogs have always been popular mascots in the navy and the coast guard. Sometimes they led patrols on foreign shores, searching for food, but mostly they were friends to sailors on long voyages far from home.

SMOKY MAY HAVE BEEN A SMALL DOG, BUT SHE HAD A BIG IMPACT ON RAISING SOLDIERS' SPIRITS.

SMOKY

But it's not just big dogs that make a difference in war. Soldiers found Smoky, a four-pound Yorkshire terrier, in a foxhole in New Guinea in World War II. Not only did she boost the spirits of lonely soldiers far from home, but she survived twelve combat missions, 150 air raids, and even a typhoon!

Dogs took an even more active role in the Vietnam War. Some 4,000 dogs were trained and shipped overseas with the US military. Dogs acted as guards and scouts in the jungle, warning their human handlers away from booby traps, land mines, and underground tunnels.

APPOLLO

NYC POLICE

K9

The navy even used dogs on patrol boats. They were trained to sniff out enemy divers and snorkelers and saved many, many lives.

In wars today, dogs are specially trained to detect hidden explosives with their powerful sense of smell (about 100,000 times better than a human's!). These dogs and their human handlers take on some of the most dangerous jobs—clearing paths through hostile territory for the soldiers to follow. They have become the military's most important tool for finding hidden bombs and land mines and keeping American soldiers safe in enemy lands. ★★★

9/11 HERO

Appollo, a German shepherd, was a member of the K-9 Unit of the New York City Police Department on September 11, 2001. Fifteen minutes after the terrorist attacks on the World Trade Center, Appollo arrived with his handler. He was almost killed by flames and pieces of the building falling from the sky, but that didn't stop him. Appollo kept searching for people to rescue. He was awarded the Dickin Medal on behalf of all the rescue dogs who helped recover victims of the attacks.

DOGS HAVE A KEEN SENSE OF SMELL THAT HELPS THEM SNIFF OUT BOMBS, FIND THE WOUNDED, AND WARN WHEN AN ATTACK IS NEAR.

HORSES ★★★

Warhorses have been used in many different ways over the centuries. Alexander the Great trained his horses and his horsemen to win countless battles. Later, in medieval times, knights rode them in wars and in contests. In the United States, horses have taken part in every war since the American Revolution.

It was George Washington who started the American **cavalry** during the Revolutionary War after losing more than one battle to the British, who had horsemen among their ranks. He himself had many horses throughout the war and was a fine horseman.

At the beginning of the Civil War, the South had many more horses and horsemen than the North. The North had to catch up or risk losing the war. Horses not only carried supplies and wounded soldiers, but also proved to be an important weapon.

ROBERT E. LEE

ROBERT E. LEE (ABOVE) AND GEORGE WASHINGTON (LEFT) WERE BOTH EXPERT HORSEMEN WHO KNEW THE IMPORTANCE OF CAVALRY SOLDIERS IN WARTIME.

GENERAL ULYSSES S. GRANT WAS SAID TO LIKE HORSES BETTER THAN PEOPLE.

ULYSSES S. GRANT

General Robert E. Lee, who commanded the Confederate army, was a famous horseman. His favorite horse, Traveller, was known for both his speed and his courage. General Ulysses S. Grant, who commanded the Union army at the end of the war, also had a famous horse—Cincinnati. Cincinnati is the horse Grant rode to Appomattox Court House in Virginia, when Lee surrendered to Grant on April 9, 1865, marking the end of the Civil War.

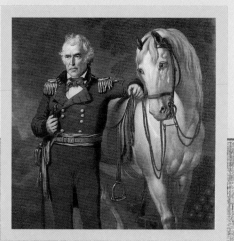

OLD WHITEY

Zachary Taylor led his men to victory in the Mexican-American War in 1848, often riding his favorite horse, Old Whitey. Taylor brought Old Whitey with him to Washington, DC, when he became president. The horse grazed on the White House lawn, but visitors kept pulling hairs from his tail for souvenirs. Taylor had to put Old Whitey in a stable to keep him safe.

WAR HORSE

A children's novel by Michael Morpurgo, War Horse, made World War I horses famous. The novel has been made into an award-winning play and a movie.

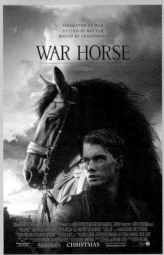

Horses also helped the United States and its allies win another war—World War I. No one knows exactly how many horses took part in the war, but there may have been as many as eight million. Not only did they carry cavalry soldiers, but they pulled heavy wagons with food and ammunition. Because of gas attacks, horses were protected with specially designed gas masks. Caring for the horses also boosted the spirits of lonely soldiers far from home. Sadly, only a few thousand horses survived the war.

By World War II, jeeps, tanks, and airplanes were more important than horses. But horses were still used in areas where tanks couldn't go—like the mountains of Italy and the jungles of Burma. After World War II, there were no more cavalry units. But horses are still a smart way for Special Forces and other small units to get around on rough terrain.

WORLD WAR II HORSES OFTEN CARRIED RADIOS AND OTHER COMMUNICATION EQUIPMENT, HELPING SOLDIERS STAY IN TOUCH WITH THEIR COMMANDING OFFICERS.

HORSES PLAYED AN IMPORTANT ROLE IN THE AMERICAN INVASION OF AFGHANISTAN. THEY CAN GO PLACES TANKS AND HUMVEES CAN NEVER REACH.

YOUR COUNTRY APPPEALS FOR **HUMANITY** JOIN THE **RED STAR** AND help to care for sick & wounded Horses in U. S. Service.

NATIONAL HEADQUARTERS, AMERICAN RED STAR ANIMAL RELIEF, ALBANY, N. Y.

AMERICAN RED STAR ANIMAL RELIEF

Most horses that took part in World War I lived for just twenty days because there were so many bullets and bombs flying around on the front lines. The Humane Association started the American Red Star Animal Relief Program to help care for sick and wounded horses.

The US Special Operations teams that led the American invasion in Afghanistan after the attacks on the World Trade Center in 2001 did so on horseback. Not only can horses travel long distances, but they also make a lot less noise than airplanes and Humvees! ★★★

BATS ★★★

When the Japanese bombed Pearl Harbor in 1941, during the Second World War, many Americans wanted to find a way to help the United States win. One man, Dr. Lytle S. Adams, came up with the idea of attaching small **incendiary** bombs to bats and dropping them over Japan from airplanes.

Bats, which can eat up to 1,000 mosquitoes a day, can carry three times their weight. Researchers believed that the bats would fly into hiding in houses and other buildings with their tiny bombs. Then they would gnaw through the strings that attached the device to their bodies and fly away before the fires started.

First the army, then the navy, and finally the marines tried to get the program, known as Project X-Ray, to work. But it turns out that bats have minds of their own. Many simply flew away, while others, unused to the weight of the bombs, fell to the ground. The project was canceled in 1944. ★★★

BATS WERE SUPPOSED TO FLY INTO ENEMY TERRITORY CARRYING TINY BOMBS, BUT THEY WOULDN'T FOLLOW ORDERS.

MADE IN JAPAN

During World War II, many Americans thought, incorrectly, that Japanese homes and factories were made of paper and wood. If that had been the case, fire-starting bats would have caused a lot of damage!

TURKEYS ★★★

TURKEYS, LOADED WITH SUPPLIES, WERE DROPPED FROM AIRPLANES FOR THE SPANISH TROOPS.

During the Spanish Civil War (1936–1939), Republicans (who supported the **democratic** government of Spain) battled the Nationalists (a **fascist** group led by General Francisco Franco).

Anarchists got involved, too, and took control of parts of southern Spain. Many Nationalists were driven into the hills, including one group that retreated to a remote monastery, a place where monks lived and worked.

The Nationalist soldiers had to be resupplied using airdrops, and someone decided it would be a good idea to use turkeys for the job. Turkeys, laden with supplies, were dropped out of planes and over the monastery.

Turkeys aren't strong flyers, but they flapped their wings as they fell, which helped slow their descent. Still, the impact of the fall killed them. When it was all over, the soldiers not only had new supplies, they also had turkey for dinner.

The Nationalists did eventually win the war, and General Franco ruled Spain for the next thirty-six years. ★★★

PIGEONS ★★★

Before the telegraph, telephone, and Internet, carrier pigeons were often the fastest way to send messages. Pigeons were used to send news of military victories as far back as ancient Greece.

When World War I broke out, armies on both sides used more than 500,000 pigeons to carry small capsules with messages, maps, photographs, and even tiny cameras to the front lines and back to headquarters. These smart birds had a 90 percent success rate!

There was more than one pigeon hero in the Great War. The most famous was a bird named Cher Ami (French for "dear friend"). The US 77th Infantry Division was stranded behind enemy lines and came under fire not just from the enemy but also from their own allies. An American officer attached a note to Cher Ami's leg telling his troops to stop firing. German troops shot at the bird, but he didn't give up. Cher Ami was blinded and shot in the breast and leg, but he still flew twenty-five miles to deliver the message and saved 194 American soldiers. Cher Ami was given France's highest military honor, the Croix de Guerre (meaning "Cross of War" or "Military Cross").

PIGEONS COULD CARRY MESSAGES AND EVEN TAKE PICTURES WITH TINY CAMERAS, LIKE THE ONE ATTACHED TO THIS BIRD.

These brave birds were called upon again in World War II. Radio communication improved between the world wars, but pigeons still played an important role. Spies and soldiers on both sides used pigeons to carry top-secret information. They were especially useful in areas where soldiers were too close to the enemy to use radios.

The army even invented a special cage and parachute for dropping pigeons from airplanes to isolated troops. The device was used to drop thousands of pigeons over France during the D-Day invasion of Normandy, in the northern part of the country. French civilians were asked to send back detailed information about German troop movements.

The D-Day attack on German troops in Europe was so secret that the Allies were allowed to communicate only through pigeons. One bird, named Gustav, flew more than 150 miles from Normandy back to England to deliver news of the first landings.

A SOLDIER PROTECTS HIS PARTNER WHO IS GETTING READY TO RELEASE A CARRIER PIGEON.

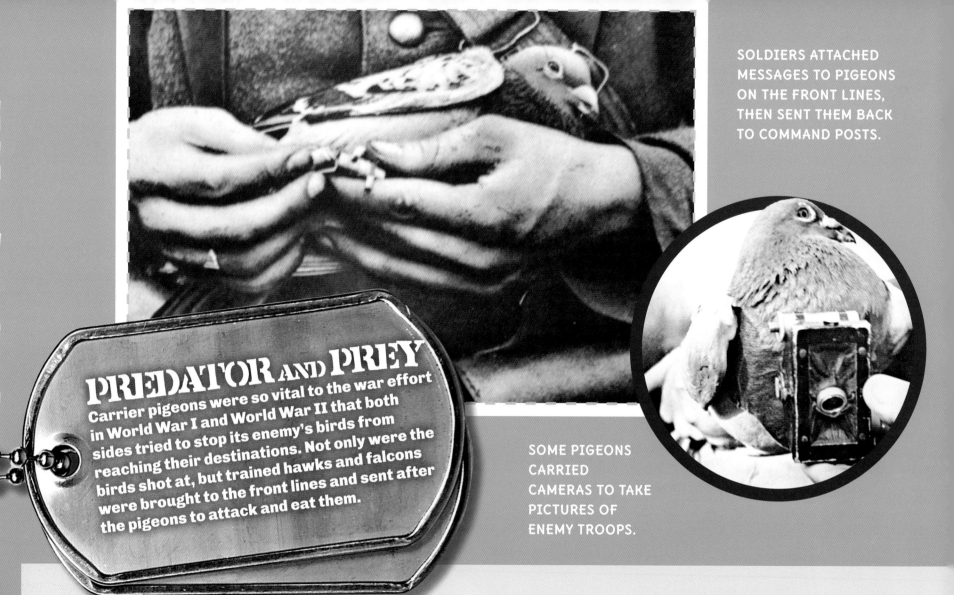

SOLDIERS ATTACHED MESSAGES TO PIGEONS ON THE FRONT LINES, THEN SENT THEM BACK TO COMMAND POSTS.

PREDATOR AND PREY

Carrier pigeons were so vital to the war effort in World War I and World War II that both sides tried to stop its enemy's birds from reaching their destinations. Not only were the birds shot at, but trained hawks and falcons were brought to the front lines and sent after the pigeons to attack and eat them.

SOME PIGEONS CARRIED CAMERAS TO TAKE PICTURES OF ENEMY TROOPS.

The most famous pigeon of World War II was named GI Joe. On October 18, 1943, an American infantry division called for heavy bombing of a German-occupied town in Italy. When the Germans retreated unexpectedly, a British brigade unknowingly moved into town shortly before the bombing was set to begin. Radio attempts to cancel the attack failed. With time running out, GI Joe was sent with the message to cancel the bombing.

GI Joe made the twenty-mile trip in just twenty minutes and arrived right as bombers were about to take off. GI Joe was awarded the Dickin Medal for gallantry, the highest award given to an animal in Great Britain. He was the only American pigeon to be honored with the medal.

Today, the pigeon service has been disbanded, but without the effort of these brave birds, the world might be a very different place. ★★★

TRAINING

World War I pigeons could fly about 200 miles in one flight. By the time World War II began, crossbreeding led to faster, stronger birds with even better homing instincts. Their average flying speed was thirty-five to forty miles per hour, but some, like GI Joe, could fly as fast as sixty mph. Carrier pigeons are bred to find their way back to their lofts, or cages. The birds were taken out on longer and longer training runs, until they could find their way home over long distances. Eight weeks after hatching, they were ready for duty.

DOLPHINS ★★★

Dolphins are among the fastest and smartest animals in the sea. No wonder these amazing creatures have served in the US Navy for more than fifty years.

In 1965, the Navy Marine Mammal Program began its first military project. A bottlenose dolphin named Tuffy dove 200 feet over and over again to carry tools to the **aquanauts** in an experimental underwater habitat called SEALAB II. He also brought mail from the aquanauts to the surface, and led lost divers to safety.

The **stealth** and speed dolphins bring to their work makes them excellent spies. They've been trained to slide through security nets and carry secret listening devices to enemy ships, and some have even learned to swim with special underwater cameras in their mouths.

Dolphins were first used in combat during the Vietnam War in the early 1970s. They patrolled the area around US ships using their echolocation (see sidebar) and let the soldiers know if they came across any suspicious swimmers.

TUFFY

WHEN NAVY DOLPHINS LIKE TUFFY FIND A MINE, THEY DROP A WEIGHTED BUOY NEAR IT SO THAT THEIR HUMAN TRAINERS CAN HANDLE IT—WITHOUT BLOWING ANYTHING UP!

THIS BOTTLENOSE DOLPHIN, NAMED K-DOG, HELPED THE NAVY FIND MINES IN THE PERSIAN GULF. THE DEVICE ON HIS FIN LETS K-DOG'S HUMAN HANDLER KNOW WHERE HE IS WHEN HE'S UNDERWATER.

In the Iraq War that began in 2003, dolphins were used to alert the US Navy to underwater mines in the Persian Gulf so that ships carrying food, medicine, and other aid could safely make their way into port.

Dolphins also help the military in home waters. In 1996, navy dolphins helped the Secret Service patrol the port of San Diego during the Republican National Convention.

ECHOLOCATION

Dolphins are able to find targets in deep, murky waters through the use of echolocation, also known as sonar. Dolphins, whales, and their relatives send out a series of sounds that bounce off of objects in the waters around them. The mammals pick up the echoes that return to them and form a picture of what's around them. This picture is much clearer than anything that can be seen by the human eye.

BELUGA WHALES

The navy has also tested whales to see what military tasks they can perform. Beluga whales, like dolphins, use sonar to find their way. The whales are able to work in much colder temperatures and at deeper depths than either dolphins or sea lions.

THE BITE PLATE IN THIS DOLPHIN'S MOUTH COULD HOLD SPY EQUIPMENT.

Today, the navy is experimenting with underwater robots that will replace its dolphin soldiers. But those machines will have to go a long way to replace the speed, sonar, and smarts of the dolphin. ★★★

SEA LIONS ★★★

CALIFORNIA SEA LIONS HAVE EXCELLENT EYESIGHT THAT ALLOWS THEM TO FIND OBJECTS AS DEEP AS 650 FEET.

Dolphins have the best sonar of all the animals used by the military, but they can't compete with the California sea lion when it comes to one important asset—their eyesight. California sea lions have amazing underwater hearing and sight. They can see clearly in dark, murky waters, even in the dead of night.

With eyesight like that, sea lions are trained by the navy to find underwater objects. They've recovered millions of dollars' worth of US naval weapons and equipment that was fired or dropped in the ocean. Sea lions can dive and recover objects as deep as 650 feet!

Sea lions are also trained to locate suspicious swimmers. They can attach a clamp or a cuff to a suspect's leg so that a security boat can reel them in like a fish. The sea lions are so fast that the person is cuffed before they know it, and the sea lion can make a fast getaway, leaving the sailors to deal with the bad guys. ★★★

THE BOYS' CLUB
The military uses only neutered male sea lions. Neutered animals are less aggressive. It also keeps their weight at a manageable 300 pounds.

HONEYBEES ★★

Can you believe that honeybees have been recruited by the military? Even the smallest creatures have been called upon to do great work.

The ancient Romans were said to sometimes **catapult** beehives into the ranks of their enemies. But in modern warfare, it's not the bees' sting, but their antennae that could defeat the enemy.

Honeybees have an amazing sense of smell. Their antennae are able to catch a whiff of pollen in the wind and track it down to a specific flower. Military scientists used this superpower to train honeybees to recognize explosives with their antennae. When they detect them, they flick their proboscis—the feeding tube that extends from their mouth—since they've been taught that they will receive sugar water as a reward.

So far, bees haven't been put to the test in the real world, but if training continues, you may soon spot a container of bees at airport security, on a subway platform, or at roadside checkpoints in a war zone. ★★★

HONEYBEES ARE TRAINED TO FLICK THEIR FEEDING TUBES WHEN THEY SMELL A BOMB.

GLOWWORMS AND GARDEN SLUGS ★★★

SOLDIERS COLLECTED THOUSANDS OF GLOWWORMS (PICTURED ABOVE) TO LIGHT THE DARK TRENCHES, LIKE THE ONE BELOW, IN WORLD WAR I.

One of the tiniest insects to ever come to a soldier's aid is the glowworm. During World War I, soldiers spent much of their time huddled in dark trenches. They would collect thousands of glowworms in jars and use their light to look over reports, study battle maps, and read letters from home.

Glowworms resemble worms, but they're really insect larvae (the young form of an insect before it transitions into an adult). They glow through a process called **bioluminescence**, which is caused by a chemical reaction in the insect. According to a 2010 study, just ten glowworms can provide the same amount of light as a streetlamp!

Glowworms weren't the only tiny creatures that helped soldiers in the trenches. Garden slugs could detect poisonous mustard gas long before humans could and curled up to protect themselves. When that happened, soldiers knew to put on their gas masks. The slugs served with US Army forces in World War I for five months, beginning in 1918, and saved many lives. ★★★

ROBO BUGS ★★★

The US military has been using robotic fliers, also known as drones, since World War II. But what about that fly you just swatted away? Was it just an insect or actually a secret listening device?

The Central Intelligence Agency (CIA) developed an "insectothopter" more than thirty years ago that looked just like a dragonfly. A tiny gasoline engine made the four wings flap, and the body contained a small listening device. But winds kept blowing the tiny bug off track, and the project was considered a failure.

Some US agencies today are experimenting with growing live insects with computer chips inside. These superbugs could follow suspects, take pictures, listen in on conversations, or even fly into bombed-out buildings to find survivors. ★★★

THE TINY, BUG-LIKE MACHINE ABOVE IS ACTUALLY A CAMERA. IT'S A LOT LESS OBVIOUS THAN A TYPICAL FLYING DRONE WITH A CAMERA, LIKE THE ONE ON THE LEFT.

PENGUINS ★★★

SIR NILS OLAV

SIR NILS OLAV INSPECTS THE TROOPS.

Most military animals merely follow orders, but there's one penguin in Scotland's Edinburgh Zoo who is a high-ranking commander in the Norwegian Royal Guard. The king penguin, named Nils Olav, has the official rank of colonel-in-chief. In 2008, he was knighted by the king of Norway, making him Sir Nils Olav.

How did this happen? The Norwegian Royal Guard regularly attends a military music festival in Edinburgh, Scotland. On one trip in 1972, a soldier visited the zoo's penguins, and his unit decided to adopt one. They named him Nils Olav.

On every following trip to Edinburgh, the Royal Guard visited their penguin and his offspring. Each time, they gave him an honorary promotion. Soon, Nils Olav outranked them all! ★★★

THE FIRST EDINBURGH PENGUINS

Norway gave the Edinburgh Zoo its first three king penguins, which were brought back from a whaling expedition in 1913.

GOATS ★ ★ ★

WILLIAM WINDSOR II

Can a goat lead soldiers to victory? In the American Revolution's Battle of Bunker Hill, a wild goat walked onto the battlefield and led a group of British soldiers up the hill to storm the American defenses. Ever since, the Royal Welch Fusiliers have had a goat for their mascot. The current mascot goat is named William Windsor II (Billy for short) and even wears a uniform!

In one US Navy legend, sailors loved a pet goat so much that they planned to have him stuffed when he died. Two officers stopped at the US Naval Academy on their way to the **taxidermist** to watch a football game. For fun at halftime, one of them put on the goatskin and ran up and down the sidelines. Navy went on to win the game, and the Naval Academy has had a goat mascot ever since.

★ ★ ★

THE NAVY MASCOT, PICTURED LEFT, ATTENDS EVERY ARMY-NAVY FOOTBALL GAME.

GLOSSARY ★★★

Allies: Countries that enter into an alliance, or agreement. In World War II, the main Allies were the United States, Great Britain, France, and the Soviet Union.

Ammunition: Bullets and shells that can be fired from a weapon

Anarchist: A person who believes in an absence of government, with no laws and complete freedom

Aquanaut: A person trained to live and work underwater for an extended period of time

Archer: A person who shoots with a bow and arrow

Bioluminescence: The chemical ability of a living being to produce its own light

Catapult: A military machine that could hurl large stones or other missiles, like beehives, at an enemy target

Cavalry: Soldiers who fight on horseback

Communism: A system of government that values the good of society over the good of individuals

Crossbreeding: Producing a superior animal or plant from two different species or from the strongest members of one species

Democracy: A government in which the people are in charge and vote for their leaders

Draft: To call into military service

Fascism: A government led by one person who has complete control

Homing: An animal's ability to return to a place after traveling a great distance away from it

Humvee: A type of military automobile that can drive on rough ground

Incendiary: An object designed to start fires

Mascot: An animal that is supposed to bring good luck to a group or a team

Migrate: To move from one area or habitat to another, often in response to the change of seasons

Neuter: To make it impossible for an animal to have offspring

Primate: A member of the biological order that includes humans, monkeys, and apes. Primates have hands and hand-like feet.

Skirmish: A short battle

Stealth: Secret, careful, and sly movements

Taxidermist: An expert in the process of preserving the skins of animals and of stuffing and mounting them in lifelike form

Terrorist: A person or organization that uses violence and fear to try to get what they want

Tour: A period of military duty

INDEX ★★★